Emotional Intelligence

The Essential Guide to Mastering Emotions

Table of Contents

Chapter 1. Introduction

Welcome to an enlightening journey that is bound to better every aspect of your life! Our Special Report, "Emotional Intelligence: The Essential Guide to Mastering Emotions", offers a roadmap to empathize with your emotions, discern them and apply that knowledge in enhancing your professional and personal life, facilitating nourishing relationships, and boosting overall well-being. Discover this all-important but widely underrated element of human intelligence and experience the joyous transformation as you read through. But, why just learn about it when you can truly master it? Yes, you heard it right! Dive into this riveting guide packed with engaging insights, practical guidance, and effective strategies that will be your companion in this pleasing voyage of self-discovery and mastery. It's time to take control of your emotional world - your adventure awaits!

Chapter 2. Understanding Emotional Intelligence

Relentless waves of emotions ebb and flow within us throughout our lives. They chart an ongoing narrative that reflects our personality, prompts our actions, and forms the groundwork for our interactions. Emotion is an inextricable aspect of our existence; navigating it intelligently opens roads to an enhanced life.

2.1. Defining Emotional Intelligence

So, what does 'emotional intelligence' entail? Coined by psychologists Peter Salovey and John D. Mayer in 1990, 'Emotional Intelligence', or EI, is the "ability to identify, use, understand, and manage emotions in positive ways to alleviate stress, communicate effectively, empathize with others, overcome challenges, and defuse conflict".

In simpler terms, EI is about recognizing and understanding not only your emotions but also those of others, and using this awareness to manage yourself and your relationships successfully.

2.2. Four Pillars of Emotional Intelligence

Modelled by psychologist Daniel Goleman, Emotional Intelligence rests on four core competencies:

1. Self-awareness: This involves recognizing and understanding your emotions as they occur and as they evolve. It also includes understanding how your emotions influence your thoughts, decisions, and behaviors. Those with profound self-awareness are attuned to their emotional triggers and can handle emotional swings effectively.

2. Self-management: Once you're aware of your emotions, managing them is the next step. This includes expressing your feelings honestly and suitably, maintaining control during stressful situations, being adaptable and open, and displaying honesty and integrity.

3. Social awareness: This involves the aptitude to sense, comprehend, and react to others' emotions while understanding social networks. Empathy plays a big role here – recognizing and understanding the feelings and perspectives of others, and taking an active interest in their needs and concerns.

4. Relationship Management: The ability to develop and maintain good relationships, communicate clearly, inspire and influence others, manage conflict, and work well in a team are crucial. This aspect of EI requires the successful application of all other areas.

2.3. Biological Basis of Emotional Intelligence

Understanding the neuroanatomy of emotional intelligence provides necessary grounding. At its most basic, emotion begins with a stimulus, processed in the brain, leading to physiological responses and subjective feelings.

The limbic system, primarily comprising the amygdala, the hippocampus, and the regions of the neocortex, plays an instrumental role. The amygdala is involved in the appraisal and recognition of emotion, and determining the emotional significance of a stimulus. The hippocampus attaches memories to emotional responses. Intertwined, they help us make sense of emotionally charged situations based on our past experiences.

The prefrontal cortex, or PFC, responsible for executive functions such as decision-making, cognitive behavior, personality expression, and social behavior, interplays with this emotional processing. For high EI, this 'emotional' brain and 'rational' brain need to work harmoniously together.

2.4. The Importance of Emotional Intelligence

Knowing what Emotional Intelligence is and appreciating its psychological and biological basis leads to the question, "Why is it important?" In essence, EI forms the bedrock of both personal and professional success. High emotional intelligence leads to better stress management, higher self-regulation, improved relationships, and enhanced communication. In the workplace, EI aligns with essential skills like teamwork, decision-making, leadership, and resilience.

Furthermore, studies demonstrate a positive correlation between EI and mental health, with those displaying higher emotional intelligence less likely to suffer from certain mental health disorders. Similarly, EI has links to physical health – capable emotion regulation strategies result in lesser physiological wear and tear in response to stress.

2.5. Building Your Emotional Intelligence: A Journey Into Self

The most empowering attribute about emotional intelligence is that it can be developed. And like any odyssey of development, it starts from within – Self-awareness.

Becoming self-aware requires self-exploration: introspecting on your emotions, how and when you feel them, why you feel the way you do, your responses and their patterns. This comes with patience, honesty, and a non-judgmental mindset towards yourself. Awareness of self is the steadfast cornerstone on which the rest of your EI is built.

2.6. Strengthening the Pillars

Once self-awareness is embodied, the other pillars can be augmented deliberately.

Self-management embraces mastery over your responses to emotions. It starts with the awareness of your emotional triggers, followed by mindfulness which slows down reactions and widens the choice of responses. Techniques like meditation, controlled breathing, and progressive muscle relaxation can be beneficial.

Social awareness is fostered by expanding your scope of empathy. It's about tuning into and understanding people's feelings. Active listening, maintaining eye contact, being responsive, and displaying empathy in conversations are helpful tools.

Relationship management is the natural outcome of combining self-awareness, self-management, and social-awareness. Good relationships are built on trust and understanding. For such connections to flourish, show genuine interest in other's feelings, be open with yours, communicate effectively, and embrace conflict resolution rather than conflict avoidance.

In conclusion, Emotional Intelligence is an ongoing journey, not a destination. It involves continuously learning, addressing challenges, and growing. Each interaction and every moment of introspection bring you one step closer to taking control of your emotional world. Here's to fostering this profoundly human intelligence. Indeed, the adventure awaits!

Chapter 3. The Science behind Emotions and Their Impact on Our Lives

Emotions, broadly speaking, are our body's responses to significant events, designed to help us respond in ways that keep us safe and well. Far more than simply expressions of our inner states of being, emotions are complex reactions involving our bodies, minds, and conscious experiences.

3.1. Unfolding the Science of Emotions

Emotions could be aptly described as a kind of barometer, measuring our interaction with events within our environments. The body's distinctive faculties respond to events that are important to us on a personal level - such as something we love, something that makes us angry, something we feel guilty about, or anything that might create fear, anxiety, or joy. The entirety of our body prepares us to deal with these important situations, manifesting itself as visible behaviors and physiological changes we recognize as emotions.

Modern science considers emotions as multi-faceted experiences as they are derived from numerous neural and physiological reactions that stimulate emotional experiences, facial expressions, and certain behaviors. Paul Ekman, a psychologist renowned for his work on emotions, identified six main universal emotions experienced by human beings - fear, anger, disgust, sadness, happiness, and surprise - although subsequent research argues that there could be numerous others.

3.2. Impact of Emotions on Behavior

Our emotional reactions don't just change our bodies or reflect on our faces - they also have a strong impact on our behaviors. For instance, if we're feeling disgust because of the rotten food, we don't only feel nauseous or make a distinct facial expression, but we also throw away the food. Similarly, feelings of joy may provoke us to seek out similar situations that provide the same positive emotional boosts. Emotions, therefore, are truly powerful motivators of behavior.

3.3. Emotions and Health

Emotions, especially when they are extreme or not properly managed, can also have a profound impact on physical health. Chronic stress, often accompanied by negative emotions like worry and anxiety, has been linked to a multitude of health issues including heart disease, diabetes, and a weakened immune system among others. On the other hand, positive emotions like happiness, love, and excitement, are correlated with a longer lifespan and better overall health. Several studies demonstrate that our emotions, and the way we deal with them, can influence our well-being quite substantially.

3.4. Brain and Emotions

When exploring the science behind emotions, it's imperative to comprehend the important role the brain plays as the epicentre of our emotional experiences. Key structures in the brain include the amygdala, hypothalamus, hippocampus, anterior cingulate cortex, and prefrontal cortex - all of which are instrumental in the generation and experience of emotions.

The amygdala, for example, plays a significant role in the detection of emotionally significant events and the triggering of an emotional response. The prefrontal cortex, on the other hand, appears particularly important in down-regulating these initial responses, helping us control our emotions.

While we traditionally associate emotions with the heart, the reality is that it's our brain that plays a central role in the formation and processing of our emotional responses.

3.5. Emotion Regulation and its Significance

Regulating our emotions aids in interacting with others, achieving our goals, and maintaining our overall well-being. It involves processes like selecting situations that make us feel certain emotions (like choosing to watch a comedy to feel happy), altering the situation to change our emotional response (like leaving a party if it's making us feel anxious), distracting ourselves, reinterpreting the event, and trying to suppress our emotional displays.

Recognizing and understanding emotions is crucial, but this must be coupled with effective methods to handle these emotions - especially the intense and unpleasant ones. Being able to do this allows us to be more resilient in the face of adversities, helps prevent burnouts and other emotional issues, and aids in maintaining and forming healthier social relationships.

Studying emotions, therefore, is not merely an academic endeavor. It is essentially about understanding the basic human experience and learning to use this profound knowledge towards evolving ourselves into emotionally intelligent individuals. Through better emotion management, we can improve our situations, relationships, and overall well-being.

The impact of emotions on our lives is far-reaching and pervasive. By fully understanding their nature, sources, and effects, we can become more adept at handling our emotional self, making our journey through life more rich, enlightened, and fulfilling. Whether in sadness or joy, fear or excitement, our emotions shape our world, driving us, and making us human.

Chapter 4. The Five Pillars of Emotional Intelligence: A Deep Dive

Emotional intelligence is intrinsically connected to five crucial elements, akin to the pillars supporting a regal monument. These pillars are self-awareness, self-regulation, motivation, empathy, and social skills. Taking a comprehensive view of these elements helps us understand what emotional intelligence truly entails. This section details each pillar and provides tangible guidance on how to cultivate each one effectively and efficiently.

4.1. Self-awareness

Self-awareness is foundational to emotional intelligence. It speaks to one's understanding of their emotions and their influence on thoughts, decisions, and behaviors. It is the ability to recognize one's strengths, weaknesses, values, and impact on others.

An exercise in boosting self-awareness is to journal your emotions. Write about experiences that triggered strong emotions in you and your reaction to these triggers. Doing so provides a recorded history that you can reflect upon and identify patterns of reactions. It gives you a deeper understanding of what pushes your buttons and how you respond.

4.2. Self-regulation

Self-regulation relates to one's ability to control emotions and impulses, enabling thoughtful responses rather than emotional reactions. It involves being comfortable with change, keeping disruptive emotions in check, and setting standards for personal conduct.

An effective strategy for cultivating self-regulation revolves around mindfulness meditation. Mindfulness involves being fully present in the moment without making judgments. It is accepting experiences as they occur without labelling them as good or bad. A simple daily mindfulness routine can reinforce emotional control.

4.3. Motivation

In the context of emotional intelligence, motivation goes beyond external rewards. It refers to a drive to achieve for the sake of achievement. It involves being action-oriented, showing commitment, and taking initiative.

To fuel your motivational engine, set self-directive goals aligned with your personal growth areas. Breaking larger goals into smaller, manageable tasks can achieve a series of small successes and keep your motivation high.

4.4. Empathy

Empathy is the ability to recognize, understand, and share the feelings of others. It extends beyond sympathy, which is feeling for someone, to feeling with someone. Empathy creates deep, personal connections and facilitates better communication which is essential in every relationship.

To develop empathy, practice active listening. This means fully focusing on the other person, avoiding interruptions, and responding thoughtfully. It also involves tuning in to non-verbal cues such as body language and facial expressions which often convey more about feelings than words.

4.5. Social Skills

The final aspect, social skills, pertains to interactions and relationships with others. Persons with refined social skills are excellent communicators, good at managing disputes, experts at fostering and maintaining relationships, and skilled at leading, influencing, and inspiring others.

Expand your social skillset by starting with improving one aspect at a time - for instance, communication. Focus on clear, concise, and considerate (the 3Cs) communication. Keep enhancing by adding conflict management, negotiation skills, and effective team collaboration to your practice.

Understanding these five pillars is the first step towards mastering emotional intelligence. Building on this knowledge requires persistent practice, personal reflection, and an open mind towards change and growth. Indeed, the path to emotional intelligence mastery is a rewarding journey that paves the way to fulfilled life experiences.

Chapter 5. Mastering Self-Awareness and Self-Regulation

The first step towards emotional intelligence is developing a deep understanding of oneself, primarily through self-awareness and self-regulation. This process requires examining our thoughts, feelings, motivations, and reactions critically and in real-time. Both self-awareness and self-regulation are interconnected and cater significantly to building emotional intelligence.

5.1. Understanding Self-Awareness

Self-awareness is the ability to recognize and understand personal moods, emotions, and drives, as well as their effects on others. It involves the knowledge of your strengths and weaknesses, your beliefs and values, your likes and dislikes, and your needs and desires. Surprisingly, many people lack self-awareness despite its importance.

Developing self-awareness involves introspection and reflection. Regular self-evaluation can help you identify patterns in your thoughts and behaviors, and the emotions driving them. This process may involve journaling about your feelings or seeking feedback from trusted friends or mentors.

Awareness of one's emotional state can help you navigate through complex situations. It can provide valuable insights into understanding not only yourself but how others perceive you. An accurate understanding of Self can result in higher confidence, better decision-making skills, and improved ability to handle stress.

5.2. Enhancing Self-Awareness

To enhance self-awareness, you can try some of the following strategies:

1. **Mindfulness Practices:** Mindfulness is present-centered awareness. Dedicated time spent in mindfulness meditation can facilitate identifying and understanding our emotions and thoughts as they arise.

2. **Self-Reflection:** Reflecting on one's experiences critically, thinking back on reactions and emotions to specific situations can increase overall self-awareness.

3. **Seeking Feedback:** Regularly seeking feedback from others can provide a third-person perspective on our behavior, actions, and reactions, contributing substantially to our self-awareness journey.

5.3. The Role of Self-Regulation

The second pillar of emotional intelligence, self-regulation, hinges on applying your self-awareness to deftly manage your emotions. It's essentially about staying in control of your emotions and not letting them hijack your peace of mind.

Self-regulation also refers to our ability to handle disruptive impulses, manage stress effectively, and express our emotions appropriately. It involves the engagement of self-control, adaptability, and resilience against challenges.

Without self-regulation, self-awareness is incomplete. Acknowledging your emotions helps, but regulating them, knowing when to express and when to control can determine your emotional intelligence's effectiveness.

5.4. Techniques for Self-Regulation

1. **Breathing Exercises:** Deep, controlled, and mindful breathing has been proven to alleviate stress and facilitate emotional control.

2. **Pause Before Reacting:** When confronted with an emotionally charged situation, consider taking a brief pause before reacting. This "emotional pause" can provide a clearer understanding of the situation.

3. **Reframe Negative Thoughts:** The way you frame your thoughts has a significant impact on the way you feel. By challenging and reframing negative thoughts, you can shift your emotional response.

4. **Practice Emotional Detachment:** Try to detach emotionally from situations where you have no control. Preserving your emotional energy for those things that you can directly influence is a wise strategy.

5. **Regular Physical Exercise:** Not only does exercise benefit your physical health, but it also helps in the management of emotions, promoting a sense of well-being and aiding in better emotional regulation.

5.5. The Interplay of Self-Awareness and Self-Regulation

Understanding the interplay between self-awareness and self-regulation is essential in reaping the benefits of emotional intelligence. Self-awareness illuminates your emotional terrain, while self-regulation helps in navigating that terrain.

When you are aware of your emotional state, you can strategically choose how to respond to your emotions, a clear marker of self-regulation. Indeed, heightened self-awareness invariably nurtures enhanced self-regulation.

To conclude, self-awareness is not a destination, but a journey of continuous self-exploration. Similarly, self-regulation is an ongoing process of managing our emotional responses. Together, they construct the foundation for emotional intelligence, leading the way to improved mental health, successful interpersonal relationships, and overall personal growth. Therefore, invest time and efforts in mastering self-awareness and self-regulation as it's central to mastering emotional intelligence.

Chapter 6. Enhancing Emotion-based Decision Making

Many decisions we make every day, though seemingly guided by logic and reason, are influenced, at least to some extent, by our emotions. In fact, current advancements in neuroscience suggest that in the absence of emotions, we might not be capable of making decisions at all. Consequently, being aware of how emotions bias our choices is a highly valuable asset on the path to emotional intelligence.

6.1. Understanding the Role of Emotions in Decision Making

Emotions are intertwined with our cognitive processes and therefore, have a profound impact on decision-making. They serve as a kind of alarm system, alerting us to situations that require action. For instance, fear is a response to perceived threat, driving us to avoid or combat the danger. Meanwhile, joy signals that we're in a rewarding situation and encourages us to stay and enjoy it.

Prospect theory, popularized by the Nobel laureate Daniel Kahneman and his colleague Amos Tversky, suggests that, in decision-making, people are more driven to avoid losses than acquire equal gains — a bias rooted in our emotions. This bias can lead us to make decisions that are not in our best interest if we let the fear of loss dominate our calculative thinking.

Simply put, emotions are not nuisances to be swept under the rug but integral elements in our decision-making framework. Once we understand this, we can start the journey to enhance our decision-making based on emotions.

6.2. The Emotional Influence and Bias

Emotions can sometimes lead us into inaccurate judgments and irrational decisions. This can occur as a result of several bias:

1. **Loss Aversion:** As mentioned earlier, this bias refers to the tendency of preferring to avoid losses over acquiring equivalent gain.

2. **Confirmation Bias:** Here, we favor information that confirms our pre-conceptions regardless of whether they are valid.

3. **Availability Bias:** This refers to our inclination to rely more heavily upon immediate, easily recalled information instead of exploring all possible options.

4. **Halo and Horns effect:** This is where an overall impression of a person influences our feelings and thoughts about that person's character or properties.

By recognizing these biases, we can start to address them by implementing strategies and practices to improve our emotional decisions.

6.3. Strategies for Enhancing Emotion-based Decision Making

To properly make sense of our emotions, and to utilize them to make the best decisions, we can use various strategies.

1. Emotional Awareness: The first step is simply to recognize that we're feeling an emotion. Employ mindfulness and awareness to take note of physical sensations or behavior changes that could indicate you're experiencing a certain emotion.

2. **Identifying Emotions:** Once you recognize you're feeling something, try to identify what the emotion is. Labeling the emotion — whether it's joy, anger, or fear — can help you address its influence on your decisions.

3. **Applying Emotion Regulation Techniques:** There are certain techniques, like mindful breathing, cognitive restructuring or reframing that can help regulate emotional arousal levels and provide a clearer perspective for decision making.

4. **Seeking Outside Perspectives:** Sometimes our emotions can blind us to other perspectives. Peer counseling or coaching can help us see the flanks we might miss.

5. **Practicing Patience:** Hasty decisions often leave room for regret. Try not to make important decisions during the peak of emotional arousal. Always give time for emotions to stabilize before making any decision.

6. **Using Empathy:** Put yourself in others' shoes can see how it feels. This approach provides you with a chance to see the whole picture and acquire a more balanced view.

6.4. Concluding Thoughts

The power of emotional intelligence lies not in disregarding or elevating emotions above all else but in integrating them with our cognitive processes, complementing, not combating, rational thinking. As you continue to learn about your emotional responses and how they interact with your decision-making, remember that it is a process, a journey. It takes patience and practice.

In sum, emotions are not hurdles to sound decisions; understood correctly, they are guides. With attention and effort, you can enhance your emotion-based decision-making, making every choice a symbiotic blend of feelings and logic. Indeed, emotional intelligence shapes not just our decisions, but our lives, our relationships, and our world.

By mastering emotional intelligence, we become masters of our fates, captains of our souls, for in understanding our feelings, we gain control over our decisions, our actions, and thus, our lives.

Chapter 7. Building Empathy: Stepping Into Others' Shoes

Unpacking the concept of empathy is a critical first step in deciphering the art and science of emotional intelligence. It is the ability to comprehend and share another's emotions and experiences as if they were your own, a vital aspect of human connection and communication. In walking the path to building empathy, one has to recognize it as the cornerstone of emotional intelligence and commit to embedding it in every interaction.

7.1. Why Empathy Matters

Empathy is a transformative trait enclosed in the fabric of social cohesion and interpersonal connection. As social creatures, humans strive to form meaningful relationships, and empathy is a catalyst in that process. It fosters understanding and sees beyond the superficial layer of human interaction to the heart of emotions. If we consider empathy as a lens, it allows us to see, understand, and respond to the emotional world of people around us. Without this lens, we might miss out on critical interpretations, cues, and signals that allow us to connect with others on a deeper level.

Being armed with empathy benefits not only personal relationships but extends to the professional environment too. An empathetic leader, for instance, is better suited to manage teams, resolve conflict, and create a positive work climate. Empathy-driven workplaces are known to see higher morale, motivation, and productivity amongst their employees.

7.2. Understanding Different Types Of Empathy

Empathy isn't a singular concept; instead, it blankets three distinct, yet interrelated types: Cognitive empathy, Emotional empathy, and Compassionate empathy.

1. Cognitive empathy refers to our ability to identify and understand other people's emotions. It's like being a mind reader, an observer who can accurately gauge what others are thinking and feeling.

2. Emotional empathy describes our response to others' emotional states - it's about sharing the feeling. It's the heavy heart you have when a close friend loses a family member, or the excitement you experience when your colleague gets a promotion.

3. Compassionate empathy goes beyond feeling; it leads to action. When we are compassionately empathetic, we not only understand and feel the person's predicament but are also spurred to help, if needed.

7.3. Building Cognitive Empathy

Foster cognitive empathy by practicing active listening — engage fully in conversations, pay close attention to what is being communicated, give non-verbal cues of understanding, and seek clarification, if required. Developing emotional literacy can complement this effort. This involves building an emotional vocabulary to effectively communicate feelings and emotions with others.

A constructive way to hone cognitive empathy is by expanding personal experiences and perspectives. This can be done by stepping outside comfort zones, interacting with diverse individuals, traveling, or even through consuming varied forms of media.

7.4. Harnessing Emotional Empathy

Emotional empathy can be difficult to navigate as it involves sharing intense emotions, which could be negative. Thus, maintaining emotional balance and self-care is critical when nurturing emotional empathy.

Meditation and mindfulness activities can provide an emotional buffer, allowing one to experience emotions without being overwhelmed. Similarly, practicing emotional regulation can help manage emotional transfer and prevent emotional exhaustion.

7.5. Cultivating Compassionate Empathy

Compassionate empathy is the culmination of understanding and feeling, fused with the urge to alleviate another's distress. It moves us past sentiment and cognition to concrete action.

To grow compassionate empathy, focus on fostering a caring and helping attitude. Regularly engage in acts of kindness and altruism. Volunteer for causes that resonate with you, help a colleague meet a deadline, or offer assistance to a struggling neighbor. Remember, no act of compassion is too small.

7.6. Putting It All Together: Building Empathy

Now that we've inspected the individual elements of empathy, the goal is to integrate them coherently.

Never underestimate the importance of open-mindedness and flexibility in empathizing with others. A willingness to look at situations from multiple lenses can significantly enhance empathetic responses. It's also essential to practice patience in this process as moments requiring empathy often involve heightened emotions, where haste can lead to emotional misinterpretation.

As we delve deeper into mastering emotional intelligence, it is imperative to remember that empathy fuels connection. Being open to receiving as well as understanding another's emotions creates a platform for authentic relationships. So, keep practicing empathy, keep learning, keep self-reflecting, and continue the journey on to mastering emotional intelligence. Through empathy, not only do we step into another's shoes, but we also, inadvertently, step into a greater understanding of ourselves and the world around us.

Chapter 8. Improving Interpersonal Relationships with Emotional Intelligence

Without a doubt, relationships hold a profound influence on our lives. They act as a mirror, reflecting our own selves. How we manage our relationships is largely governed by our Emotional Intelligence (EI). Higher EI assists us in understanding, empathizing, and effectively responding to the emotions of those around us, thereby fortifying interpersonal relationships.

8.1. Understanding and Empathizing with Emotions

Possessing the ability to comprehend emotions, both our own and those of others, is the key to enhancing interpersonal relationships. This involves actively observing, acknowledging, and reflecting upon our emotional states and those we interact with. It encourages empathetic responses, fostering deeper connections.

Empathy is a vital component of EI. It involves not just understanding another's point of view but also sharing their feelings. There are two types: cognitive empathy (intellectually understanding a person's perspective) and emotional empathy (actually feeling what the person feels). Both types can improve interpersonal relationships when applied appropriately.

Strategies to enhance understanding and empathizing with emotions include: * Active listening: Encourages thoughtful responses and validates other people's feelings. * Open-ended inquiries: These allow for exploration of others' viewpoints. * Avoiding judgment: Creating a safe environment fosters more genuine emotion-sharing. *

Mindfulness: This encourages empathy by cultivating a non-judging awareness of present-moment experiences.

8.2. Responsively Expressing Emotions

While understanding and empathy are critical, relationships also demand expression of our own emotions. Assertive, not aggressive, expression generates positive responses, striking a balance between your needs and others' sentiments. An effective strategy is using "I" statements, which allow personal emotions to be communicated without attributing blame. For example, instead of saying, "You never listen to me", you might say, "I feel unheard when my thoughts are interrupted".

Also, acknowledgments such as "I understand" or "I see your viewpoint" are powerful validation tools. Sharing emotions asserts a sense of openness and vulnerability, increasing rapport.

8.3. Interpreting Nonverbal Communication

Nonverbal communication underscores every interpersonal interaction. Accurate interpretation helps gauge the emotional state of others. Facial expressions, body language, tone of voice, and even timing and pace of response provide vital insights. Maintaining eye contact, noting subtle changes in demeanor, and being aware of our own nonverbal cues ensure effective communication, enhancing relationships.

8.4. Handling Conflict with Emotional Maturity

Conflict is inevitable in relationships but can be managed effectively with Emotional Intelligence. Assertive expression cushions disagreements, while empathy can defuse contentious situations.

A key strategy is employing active listening during disputes, ensuring all parties feel heard. This encourages a problem-solving approach and mitigates defensive responses. A calm, assertive, and respectful demeanor when augmented with powerful tools like negotiation and compromise, turns conflicts into relationship-strengthening experiences.

8.5. Encouraging Emotional Expression among Peers

Creating an environment conducive to emotional expression results in trust and better interpersonal relationships. We can foster this by: * Encouraging colleagues to share their feelings. * Upholding emotional transparency as a team value. * Leading by example, expressing our emotions constructively. * Facilitating group activities that promote emotional sharing, such as team-building exercises.

8.6. Fostering Emotional Reliability

Being emotionally reliable makes one a trusted confidant. It means remaining consistent and dependable in emotional responses, not fluctuating wildly or reacting disproportionately. This trait puts those around us at ease, and they will likely reciprocate, mutually enhancing the bond.

8.7. The Role of Self-regulation in Relationship Success

Self-regulation, the ability to manage our own emotions, significantly impacts how we handle relationships. Those who self-regulate effectively are adaptable, open to change, and able to turn negatives into positives. They are capable of setting clear boundaries and maintaining them, contributing to balanced, healthy relationships. Techniques such as self-soothing, mindfulness, and emotion-focused coping strategies assist in honing self-regulation.

To recap, Emotional Intelligence plays an indispensable role in interpersonal relationships. It encompasses understanding, empathizing, responsive expression, nonverbal communication interpretation, conflict handling, fostering emotional expression, promoting emotional reliability, and effective self-regulation. By honing these skills, we can significantly enhance our relationships on all fronts, leading to more fulfilling interpersonal connections.

Chapter 9. Emotional Intelligence and Leadership: Leading with Heart

As we delve deeper into the intriguing world of emotional intelligence, we come to recognize its profound correlation with leadership. Emotional intelligence is not an isolated influence but rather a foundation that intersects all areas of our lives, substantially impacting our abilities to lead.

9.1. Understanding Emotional Intelligence in Leadership

Notably, leadership styles have transformed dramatically over the years. A shift from autocratic perspectives to democratic or transformational leadership is evident, acknowledging the idea that power is constructively shared. Leaders today are well-advised to understand their teams' feelings and motivations to inspire them towards their common goals. Hence, emotional intelligence emerges as an underlining trait among successful leaders harnessing empathic communication and productive interactions.

The categorization of emotional intelligence into the five dimensions of self-awareness, self-regulation, motivation, empathy, and social skills provides a comprehensive framework for understanding its utilization in leadership roles.

9.2. Self-awareness in Leadership

Self-awareness marks the beginning of emotional intelligence. As leaders, the ability to understand our emotions and how they impact our actions and decisions is of utmost importance. This understanding allows us to correctly perceive our strengths and weaknesses and to communicate clearly and confidently.

A self-aware leader is approachable, takes constructive criticism well, and exhibits flexibility in their thought processes. They can address their blind spots and constantly improve, evolving with the changing face of leadership dynamics.

9.3. Inculcating Self-regulation in Leadership Styles

Leaders equipped with self-regulation can deal with disruptive emotions calmly, creating a positive environment even in times of stress. Their decision-making process remains unaffected by personal emotions or prejudices, promoting an unbiased and just culture within the organization.

Self-regulation further helps leaders maintain standards of honesty and integrity within their teams. These benchmarks build trust and create a setting where employees feel valued and safe, significantly shooting up productivity levels.

9.4. The Role of Motivation in Emotional Intelligence

An emotionally intelligent leader leverages their intrinsic motivation to drive them towards their goals. This self-driven approach reflects in their work ethics and encourages the team to harness their inner zeal as well. Such leaders inspire by example, setting positive trends within the workplace.

These leaders can identify opportunities in adversity and stay optimistic amidst challenges, drawing everyone out of potential turbulent zones with their unwavering belief and resilience.

9.5. Empathy: The Core of Emotionally Intelligent Leadership

Emotionally intelligent leaders recognize the feelings of their team members and respond accordingly, an attribute known as empathy. Empathic leaders show genuine concern about their team's well-being, fostering a healthy work-life integration.

Such leaders respect diversity of perspective and ensure that everyone feels heard and understood. This consideration significantly enhances team relationships and promotes creativity and innovation.

9.6. Developing Social Skills: Cementing the Bond of Leadership

Solidifying relationships in a professional ecosystem is a significant component of successful leadership. Leaders with adept social skills manage their teams efficiently, troubleshoot conflicts, and catalyze change for the better.

They can recognize the emotional currents within their team, address issues proactively, and deliver praise and constructive feedback effectively. These adepts navigate the social networks within an organization, forging strong alliances and ensuring smooth functioning.

9.7. Integrating Emotional Intelligence in Leadership

Now that we understand the dimensions of emotional intelligence, the question arises - how do we integrate these facets into our leadership repertoire? Let's delve into some strategies.

9.8. Building Emotional Awareness

Fostering emotional intelligence requires an understanding and acknowledgement of emotions. Keep a journal to record emotional responses to events throughout the day. Reflecting on these observations promotes self-awareness.

9.9. Practicing Mindfulness

Mindfulness teaches us to live in the present, accepting our emotions without judgment. This practice drives self-regulation and self-awareness, crucial emotional intelligence parameters.

9.10. Improving Communication

Effective communication, the cornerstone of leadership, thrives on empathy and social skills. Regularly interacting with your team members can extend your comprehension of their emotional needs and help you frame clear, attentive responses.

9.11. Encouraging Feedback

Feedback mechanisms provide objective insights into our behavior. Constructive critique can reveal areas of improvement and help enhance emotional awareness.

9.12. Nonstop Learning

Emotional intelligence, like every other skill, demands continuous improvement and commitment. Attending workshops, reading relevant books, or hiring a coach can guide you on this journey.

In conclusion, emotional intelligence impacts every leadership decision, enriching the interactions we undertake and the relationships we foster. By integrating emotional intelligence principles into leadership fundamentals, one can not only become an effective leader but also a catalyst for positive, sustainable change. Emotional Intelligence is not just about leading with your heart – it's about leading with your heart intelligently.

Chapter 10. Practical Techniques to Boost Your Emotional Intelligence

Emotional intelligence is a crucial skillset that actively contributes to our personal and professional lives. The good news? It can be enhanced and cultivated with awareness, understanding, and practice. This chapter is a comprehensive guide presenting practical techniques that can aid in boosting emotional intelligence.

10.1. Identify Your Emotions

The first step on the road to boosting emotional intelligence is identifying your emotions. You can't manage what you can't measure. Use a journal to regularly record your feelings and thoughts.

NOTE An emotion-focused journal can help trace emotional patterns and recognize triggers.

Take note not just of the emotion, but the circumstances triggering it. Were you stressed? Fatigued? Frustrated with someone? Identifying patterns over time can be quite enlightening and provide insights into your emotional world.

10.2. Understand Your Emotions

Once you've identified your emotions, strive to understand why they occur. Dig deep and think about why certain situations trigger specific reactions in you. Use these questions to guide your exploration:

- What about this situation caused my emotional response?

- Has something similar happened before? How did I react then?

- How did my response impact the situation and those around me?

A self-reflective approach will take you towards a deeper understanding of both your emotions and yourself.

10.3. Emotional Responsiveness versus Reactiveness

Responsiveness and reactiveness are often intermingled, yet they bring about very different outcomes. Being reactive involves instinctual behavior without consideration of potential outcomes, while being responsive implies a thoughtful action to an emotional stimulus. Your goal is to lean towards responsiveness.

Reactiveness often leads to regret or external damage, responsiveness, however, leads to constructive outcomes. To shift from reactivity to responsiveness, use these strategies:

- Mindfulness: Awareness of the present moment, can help identify and choose how to respond.

- Pause Technique: Give yourself a moment before responding to an emotionally intense situation.

When an emotional storm hits you, remember: Feel, pause, then respond.

10.4. Developing Your Emotional Vocabulary

Having a rich emotional vocabulary facilitates articulating feelings accurately. This decreases instances of misunderstanding and nurtures healthy relationships. To expand your emotional vocabulary, employing the 'Feelings Wheel' could be fruitful.

The Feelings Wheel is a tool represented by a circle, comprising multiple layers illustrating a wide array of emotions. The innermost circle lists basic emotions: happy, sad, fearful, angry, surprised, and disgusted. Surrounding layers present more nuanced emotions, expanding your emotional vocabulary.

10.5. Practice Active Listening

In enhancing emotional intelligence, engaging in active listening is a powerful tool. Actively listening to someone means fully concentrating on their words, understanding their message, responding appropriately, and then remembering what has been said. Here are some techniques to practice active listening:

- Eye Contact: Show that you're engaged by maintaining eye contact.

- Nodding: Non-verbal cues like nodding express that you're understanding their points.

- Reflective Listening/Paraphrasing: Summarize or paraphrase their words in your response to assure them you understand their perspective.

10.6. Developing Empathy

Empathy, the ability to understand and share feelings of another, is a cornerstone of emotional intelligence. Displaying empathy means stepping into another's shoes to comprehend their emotions accurately. Here are some ways to develop empathy:

- Be present and attentive when interacting with others.
- Listen without interrupting.

• Validate their feelings, without judgement.

Enhanced empathy promotes positive relationships and a harmonious work environment.

10.7. Emotion Regulation

Regulating your emotions involves identifying, understanding, and managing how you respond to emotions. Techniques like deep breathing, meditation, and progressive muscle relaxation can help in emotion regulation. Regulating emotions isn't about suppressing them, but managing how and when you express them.

Developing emotional intelligence is a journey of self-discovery, growth, and transformation. Embracing the techniques presented in this chapter will fuel your journey, fostering a better understanding of yourself and others, stronger relationships, and an enriched lifestyle. Embrace this journey of self-discovery, growth, and transformation. Evolve and enjoy the world around you in its emotional richness and depth.

Chapter 11. Transforming Challenges into Growth: Emotional Resilience

The journey to emotional resilience often begins with acknowledging that life is peppered with challenges. These challenges, big and small, can either stunt our growth or be the catalyst for significant self-improvement. The differentiation lies within our approach and perspective—how we choose to perceive and respond to these challenges. This is where emotional resilience steps in to play a vital role.

11.1. Fostering an Understanding of Emotional Resilience

Emotional resilience is the ability to successfully manage and adapt to stress and adversity. It's not about avoiding problems but confronting them head-on, all while maintaining a positive outlook. It's the mental armour that helps you recuperate from life's battles with more wisdom, empathy, and grit than before. If life were a boxing match, emotional resilience would be your ability to get back up after being knocked down.

Everyone has some degree of resilience. Like many aspects of emotional well-being, our capability for resilience is not fixed; rather, it's a dynamic, evolving trait that can be developed and enhanced over time. The key attribute of emotional resilience is indeed the universal potential to cultivate it within ourselves.

11.2. Developing Emotional Awareness: The First Step to Emotional Resilience

The process of becoming emotionally resilient fundamentally starts with emotional awareness—the ability to recognize, identify, and understand one's own feelings. Recognizing the diverse array of emotions that we experience is the rudimentary step to managing them effectively.

By becoming more attuned to your emotions, you acquire a higher level of self-understanding, which provides a strong platform for developing emotional resilience. Practice mindfulness to become more aware of your emotional states. Whether it's through meditation, journaling, or merely taking a few moments to reflect on your emotional status throughout the day, enhancing your awareness is a crucial step to building emotional resilience.

11.3. Modified Perception: The Power of Positive Thinking

Our perceptions have a profound influence on how we deal with challenges. Viewing difficulties as insurmountable problems can lead to damaging outlooks and unhealthy coping mechanisms. However, by shifting our perception and seeing these challenges as opportunities for growth, we can foster a healthier outlook and avoid unnecessary stress.

This is not about neglecting the magnitude of the problems we face, but rather modifying our perception to focus on growth, rather than the impending doom of failure. It involves adopting a positive outlook and recognizing that every hardship comes cultivated with seeds of new wisdom, strength, and growth.

11.4. Problem-Solving and Emotional Control

When faced with a problem, our emotional response may either blur or clarify the path to a solution. While it's perfectly human to experience emotions like anger, sadness, or anxiety in the face of challenges, these emotions can become a hindrance when they monopolize our response.

The ability to control your emotions is key to becoming emotionally resilient. Cultivate the habit to take a moment and gain inner composure when stressed. This involves knowing when to step back, breathe, and allow your emotions to settle, so you can address the problem from a relaxed, focused state.

11.5. Cultivating Empathy to Foster Emotional Resilience

Developing empathy towards others and yourself is another vital ingredient for emotional resilience.

Empathy is a potent tool that allows us to understand and sympathize with the hardships and emotions of others. This understanding can enhance our resilience by providing new perspectives and promoting compassionate, balanced responses to challenges. When we empathize with others, we learn to be resilient by observing and learning from their solutions.

Having empathy towards oneself can also aid the cultivation of resilience. Self-empathy encourages forgiving and giving oneself the same understanding we'd extend to others confronting the same situation. Dealing with ourselves with the same level of compassion and understanding is a critical aspect of resilience and cultivates a nurturing mental environment where resilience can thrive.

11.6. The Importance of Healthy Relationships

Emotional resilience is not something we need to develop in isolation. Our relationships, being one of the most influential factors in our lives, are a prevalent catalyst contributing to our resilience. Supportive relationships encourage emotional well-being and provide a safe space to express and understand difficult emotions.

It's important to surround yourself with people who understand and respect your feelings and can provide different perspectives and emotional support when needed. Sharing your struggles or victories with trusted friends, family, or mentors can boost your resilience by offering extra layers of support and perspective.

11.7. Physical Health: The Ignored catalyst

Emotional well-being is often intricately tied with physical health. Regular exercise, a balanced diet, and sufficient sleep can have profound impacts on your mental state, and thus, your resilience. Exercise, in particular, triggers the release of endorphins, which act as natural mood lifters.

The journey to emotional resilience is an ongoing process. It is not a destination but a path, a set of habits, and lifestyle choices that facilitate emotional well-being and growth. Emotional resilience can be seen as a tapestry, interwoven with the threads of emotional awareness, positive thinking, emotional self-control, empathy, supportive relationships, and physical health. Cultivate these habits and watch how your previously insurmountable challenges transform into significant stepping-stones of growth. In the agitated storm of life, let the cultivation of emotional resilience be your unwavering anchor. Remember, your growth story is not defined by the obstacles you face but the resilience you foster.

www.ingramcontent.com/pod-product-compliance
Lightning Source LLC
Chambersburg PA
CBHW071008260726
48661CB00007B/2853